BLOGGING

Your Path to Success (A Comprehensive Guide to Thriving in the Digital World)

Ali Muattar

ANish Publications

ANISH
PUBLICATIONS

First Edition: 2016
Second Edition: 2020
Third Edition: 2025
Cover Design: ANish Designs
Publisher: ANish Publications
Published in the Islamic Republic of Pakistan

Disclaimer:

The information provided in this book is for general informational purposes
only. While the author has made every effort to ensure the accuracy and
completeness of the information, the author assumes no responsibility
for errors, omissions, or inaccuracies. Any reliance you place on such
information is strictly at your own risk. The author will not be liable for any
loss or damage arising from the use of this book.

Trademarked names, logos, and images mentioned in this
book are the property of their respective owners and are
used here for identification purposes only.

This book is dedicated to all blogger out there who are trying their best to educate inform and entertain public worldwide. Thanks for being here your contributions to the world of blogging and informed public is worthy of dedicating this book to you. Be always brave to say what is necessary and important for world to listen.

Blogging is the shortest path to show the world what you have and how to shine in your skin.

-ALI MUATTAR

CONTENTS

FOREWORD

In an era where our lives are seamlessly interfered with the digital world, the art of blogging has emerged as a profound tool for expression, connection, and impact. It is my honor to introduce you to "Blogging: Your Path to Success," a comprehensive guide crafted by Ali Muattar, a true blogger in the world of online influence.

Ali's journey, from a passionate blogger to a respected entrepreneur, has been inspiring evidence to the potential that is within the world of blogging. With every word he pens and every insight he shares, he opens the door to a universe of limitless possibilities.

As you look into the pages of this book, you'll discover that it's more than just a guide; it's a roadmap to not only surviving but thriving in the digital world. Ali's meticulous attention to detail, combined with his deep understanding of the nuances of blogging, ensures that every reader, regardless of their background, will find invaluable guidance.

"Blogging: Your Path to Success" isn't just about creating content; it's about mastering the art of storytelling, building an engaged audience, and turning your passion into a purposeful venture. Ali's dedication to empowering others shines through every chapter, providing a steady hand to navigate the challenges and seize the opportunities that wait.

Whether you're a newcomer looking to enter into your blogging journey or an experienced blogger aiming to refine your craft, this book holds the keys to unlocking your potential. Prepare to be equipped with the tools, knowledge, and inspiration needed to make your mark in the ever evolving world of blogging.

It's with great pleasure that I invite you to immerse yourself in these pages. As you absorb Ali's insights, remember that you're not just reading a book; you're going through on a transformational experience that has the power to shape your digital destiny.

Congratulations on taking the first step toward your path to blogging success.

Warm regards,

Ali W.

Author, "Writing Everything For Success"

INTRODUCTION

In an age defined by digital connectivity, the power of words has transcended traditional boundaries, finding its haven in the vast expanse of the online world. The journey of a blogger is a journey of transformation – from an individual with a message to a creator who can influence, inspire, and impact lives. Welcome to "Blogging: Your Path to Success," a guide designed to unlock the doors to this exciting and limitless world.

The heartbeat of this book pulses with the belief that every individual possesses a unique voice and perspective that can contribute to human expression. Whether you're a seasoned writer seeking to amplify your voice or a curious newcomer stepping onto this digital stage, "Blogging: Your Path to Success" is your compass, your mentor, and your confidant on this exhilarating voyage.

Blogging isn't just about writing; it's about exploring narratives that resonate, sparking conversations that matter, and connecting with a global community hungry for knowledge, entertainment, and inspiration. As you navigate the chapters that follow, you'll discover a treasure of insights, strategies, and anecdotes that will guide you through the multifaceted world of blogging.

From defining your niche to crafting compelling content, from building an audience to monetizing your passion – every facet of the blogging journey is dissected and illuminated. You'll not only gain a tactical understanding of the tools available to you but also develop a strategic mindset that propels you toward success.

However, remember that success in blogging isn't measured solely by numbers or accolades; it's defined by the impact you have on your readers, the connections you forge, and the legacy you build. It's about the stories you share, the problems you solve, and the conversations you spark. As you immerse yourself in these pages, absorb the wisdom, but also cultivate your individuality – for it's in embracing your authenticity that you'll truly shine.

This book is more than a guide; it's a declaration of the potential within you. As you travel on this journey, carry with you the knowledge that your words have the power to shape perceptions, influence decisions, and change lives. "Blogging: Your Path to Success" is your companion, your roadmap, and your catalyst for making your mark in the digital universe.

Get ready to embrace your role as a storyteller, a thought leader, and a change maker. Your path to success begins here.

Warm regards,

Ali Muattar
Author, "Blogging: Your Path to Success"

PREFACE

Welcome to "Blogging: Your Path to Success." As you hold this book in your hands, you're starting on a journey that I hope will not only inform and inspire you but also ignite your passion for the transformative world of blogging.

Throughout my journey as a blogger and entrepreneur, I've witnessed the incredible power of the digital world. I've seen ordinary individuals harness their creativity, share their stories, and turn their blogs into influential platforms that shape industries and change lives. It's this potential for transformation that led me to write this comprehensive guide.

In these pages, you'll find not only practical tips and techniques but also the underlying psychology that drives successful blogging. From finding your niche to establishing your authority, each chapter is designed to provide you with the tools and knowledge you need to thrive.

I've poured my heart and soul into "Blogging: Your Path to Success." I've drawn from personal experiences, both triumphs, and challenges, to offer you a holistic understanding of what it take to flourish as a blogger. Whether you're just starting or seeking to elevate your existing skills, this book is meant to accompany you every step of the way.

Remember, blogging is more than just crafting words on a screen. It's about connecting with others, sharing your unique perspective, and building a community that resonates with your message. As you look into the following chapters, keep your aspirations at the forefront of your mind and let your dedication drive your journey.

Thank you for choosing to be a part of this adventure. I'm excited to join you on the path to blogging success.

Warm regards,

Ali Muattar

Author, "Blogging: Your Path to Success"

CHAPTER 1: INTRODUCTION TO BLOGGING

The Evolution of Blogging

Understanding the Modern Blogging World

Why Blogging Matters in Today's Digital Age

Introduction To Blogging

In the digital age, blogging has emerged as a powerful and accessible platform for individuals and businesses to share their thoughts, expertise, and experiences with a global audience. A blog, short for "weblog", is essentially an online journal or informational website that presents content in a chronological format, with the most recent posts appearing at the top. Blogs cover a wide range of topics, from personal diaries to professional insights, entertainment, travel, lifestyle, technology, and much more. This introduction will provide you with a comprehensive overview of blogging, its benefits, and the essential components of starting and maintaining a successful blog.

Benefits of Blogging

Expression and Creativity: Blogging offers a creative outlet for individuals to express their thoughts, ideas, and opinions. It allows writers to develop their unique voice and style.

Knowledge Sharing: Blogs are an excellent platform for sharing knowledge and expertise on specific subjects. Whether you're an expert in a particular field or a passionate hobbyist, you can educate and inform your audience.

Building a Community: Blogs can foster a sense of community around shared interests. Readers can engage with the content through comments, likes, and social media shares, creating a dialogue between the writer and the audience.

Personal Branding: For professionals, blogging can contribute to personal branding. Sharing insights and industry knowledge can establish you as a thought leader in your field, potentially leading to new opportunities.

Monetization: Successful blogs can be monetized through various methods such as advertising, sponsored content, affiliate marketing, and selling digital products or services.

Components of a Successful Blog

Content: High quality, engaging, and relevant content is the heart of a successful blog. Your writing should resonate with your target audience and provide value to them.

Design and Experience: A clean and friendly design is crucial for keeping readers engaged. Ensure that your blog is visually appealing, easy to navigate, and responsive across different devices.

Domain Name and Hosting: Choose a memorable domain name that reflects the theme or focus of your blog. Hosting is the service that allows your blog to be accessible on the internet.

Platform: Select a blogging platform that suits your needs. Popular options include WordPress, Blogger, and Medium. These platforms provide friendly interfaces for creating and managing your blog.

Frequency and Consistency: Regular updates keep your audience engaged and coming back for more. Decide on a posting schedule that you can realistically maintain, whether it's daily, weekly, or monthly.

Engagement: Interact with your readers by responding to comments and fostering discussions. Encourage social media sharing to increase your blog's reach.

Search Engine Optimization (SEO): Optimize your blog posts for search engines to increase your chances of being discovered by a wider audience. Use relevant keywords, meta descriptions, and proper formatting.

Analytics: Monitor your blog's performance using analytics tools. This helps you understand your audience's preferences, track traffic, and make informed decisions to improve your blog's effectiveness.

Blogging has evolved into a versatile medium that enables individuals and businesses to communicate, share, and connect with a global audience. By understanding the benefits of blogging and mastering the key components of creating and maintaining a successful blog, you can effectively contribute your voice to the online world while building a community of engaged readers. Whether you're pursuing personal expression, professional growth, or a combination of both, blogging offers a powerful platform to achieve your goals.

The Evolution Of Blogging

Blogging has come a long way since its inception in the late 1990s. From its early days as simple online diaries to its current status as a diverse and influential form of online content, the evolution of blogging reflects the changing world of technology, communication, and culture. Let's explore the key phases in the evolution of blogging:

Emergence (Late 1990s Early 2000s)

Origins: The term "weblog" was first coined in 1997, referring to a website that maintained a log of links and commentary.

Personal Diaries: Blogs initially served as personal online diaries, where individuals shared their thoughts, experiences, and daily lives.

Manual Coding: Bloggers often had to code their blogs manually using HTML, and updates required technical skills.

Rise of Platforms (Mid2000s)

Friendly Platforms: Platforms like Blogger (1999) and later Word-Press (2003) made blogging more accessible by offering friendly interfaces and templates.

Diverse Topics: Blogs expanded beyond personal diaries to cover a wide range of topics, including news, politics, technology, fashion, and lifestyle.

Community Building: Blog rolls, comments sections, and trackbacks enabled interaction and community building among bloggers and readers.

Mainstream Adoption (Late 2000s Early 2010s)

Professionalization: Blogging transitioned from a hobby to a profession for many, with bloggers earning income through ads, sponsored content, and affiliate marketing.

Corporate and Media Blogs: Businesses and media organizations recognized the potential of blogs for branding, engagement, and content marketing.

Micro blogging: Platforms like Twitter introduced micro blogging, condensing content into short posts and challenging traditional long form blogging.

Social Media Integration (Mid2010s)

Social Sharing: Social media platforms became integral to blogging, allowing bloggers to share content quickly and engage with readers on multiple channels.

Visual Content: The rise of platforms like Instagram and Pinterest led to an increased focus on visual content and storytelling.

Content Diversity and Multimedia (Late 2010s Present)

Video and Podcasting: Bloggers started incorporating video content through platforms like YouTube and podcasting through platforms like Apple Podcasts and Spotify.

Niche Blogging: Specialized niches gained popularity as bloggers focused on specific interests and built dedicated audiences.

Long Form Content: Despite the rise of short form content, long form blogging persisted, offering in-depth analysis, tutorials, and comprehensive guides.

Evolution of Platforms and Formats (Present and Beyond)

Platform Diversification: New platforms, such as Medium and Substack, offer alternative ways for writers to share their content and monetize their work.

Interactive Content: Interactive elements, such as quizzes, polls, and interactive infographics, enhance engagement.

AI Integration: AI tools are being used to assist bloggers in content generation, editing, and optimizing for SEO.

Blogging's evolution reflects the dynamic nature of the internet and communication. From personal diaries to professional content creation, blogging has adapted to changing technologies and preferences. As technology continues to advance, blogging will likely continue to transform, shaping the way we share information, connect with others, and express ourselves in the digital age.

Understanding The Modern Blogging World

The modern blogging world has evolved significantly in response to technological advancements, changing behaviors, and shifts in content consumption preferences. As we delve into the contemporary blogging environment, it's crucial to recognize the key trends, challenges, and opportunities that define the present state of blogging:

Blogs have expanded beyond traditional text based posts to include various content formats, such as videos, podcasts, infographics, and interactive content. Multimedia content appeals to different learning styles and engages audiences across various platforms, enhancing the overall experience. Niche blogging has gained prominence as content creators focus on specific, targeted topics that cater to passionate and engaged audiences. Specialized blogs tend to attract more loyal readers who are seeking in-depth expertise and insights.

Social media platforms play a crucial role in distributing and promoting blog content to a wider audience. Influencer collaborations, partnerships, and cross promotions help bloggers extend their reach and connect with new readers. Bloggers are using social media not only to share their content but also to engage directly with their audience, fostering community and conversation. Platforms like Instagram, Twitter, and TikTok enable bloggers to showcase their personality and connect on a more personal level.

Search engine optimization (SEO) remains a vital aspect of blogging, ensuring that content is discoverable by search engines and attracts organic traffic. Bloggers are adapting to evolving SEO practices, such as voice search optimization and mobile friendly design. Bloggers have diversified their revenue streams beyond traditional advertising to include affiliate marketing, sponsored content, digital products, online courses, and premium subscriptions. Monetization strategies are tailored to the blogger's audience, content type, and expertise.

Personalization tools and AI-driven recommendations enhance experiences by delivering content tailored to individual preferences and behaviors. Bloggers are leveraging data analytics to better understand their audience and create more relevant content. Many bloggers have integrated ecommerce elements, directly selling products related to their niche or partnering with brands to offer exclusive merchandise. This trend blurs the line between content creation and online retail.

With the majority of internet s accessing content on mobile devices, bloggers prioritize responsive design and mobile optimization for seamless experiences. Bloggers are increasingly conscious of ethical considerations, including transparency about affiliate relationships, responsible product endorsements, and environmental sustainability. Data privacy concerns have led bloggers to adopt stronger security measures, particularly if they collect data or engage in ecommerce.

The modern blogging world is a dynamic ecosystem that reflects the evolving preferences of readers and the rapid advancement of technology. Bloggers must adapt to changing trends, embrace various content formats, and engage with their audience across multiple platforms. By staying attuned to the latest developments, bloggers can continue to thrive in this dynamic environment while providing valuable content and building meaningful connections with their readers.

Why Blogging Matters In Today's Digital Age

Blogging continues to hold significant relevance in today's digital age, playing a pivotal role in shaping online communication, information dissemination, and personal and professional growth. Here are several compelling reasons why blogging matters in the current digital world:

Blogging offers a platform for individuals to express their thoughts, opinions, and expertise on a wide range of topics. It fosters creativity and allows writers to develop their unique voice, contributing to a diverse online discourse. Blogs serve as valuable educational resources, enabling experts to share their insights, tips, and knowledge with a global audience. Readers can access tutorials, guides, and in-depth analyses that help them learn and grow in various fields.

Blogging positions individuals and businesses as thought leaders in their respective industries. Consistently sharing valuable, insightful content builds credibility and authority, which can lead to new opportunities and collaborations. Blogs create a sense of community by allowing readers to engage through comments, shares, and discussions. Bloggers can form meaningful connections with likeminded individuals and foster dialogue on important topics.

Blogs enhance a website's search engine optimization (SEO) by regularly providing fresh, relevant content. Well optimized blog posts increase the chances of being discovered by search engines and attracting organic traffic. Blogging encourages self-reflection and personal development as writer's research, articulate ideas, and refine their communication skills. For professionals, blogging can lead to career advancement, networking, and job opportunities.

Blogs can generate income through various monetization strategies, such as advertising, affiliate marketing, sponsored content, and selling digital products. Many bloggers have turned their blogs into successful online businesses. Blogs allow individuals to share their stories, experiences, and journeys in a multimedia rich format. Personal narratives and anecdotes create relatable and engaging content that resonates with readers.

High quality, well researched blogs can serve as reliable sources of information in an era of misinformation and fake news. Bloggers who prioritize accuracy and credibility contribute to a more informed online environment. Blogging has adapted to changing digital trends, including the rise of social media, mobile devices, and multimedia content. Bloggers who embrace new technologies and formats remain relevant and effective in engaging their audience.

Blogging remains a cornerstone of the digital age, offering a platform for individuals and businesses to share their perspectives, educate, connect, and contribute to the online world. In a world characterized by rapid information exchange, blogging serves as a valuable medium for meaningful communication, personal development, and professional success. As technology continues to evolve, blogging will likely continue to evolve alongside it, maintaining its significance in shaping the way we communicate and interact online.

CHAPTER 2:
FINDING YOUR
BLOGGING NICHE

Identifying Your Passion and Expertise

Researching and Evaluating Potential Niches

Choosing the Perfect Niche for Long-term Success

Finding Your Blogging Niche

Selecting the right niche is a crucial step in starting a successful blog. Your chosen niche defines the focus and direction of your content, helping you attract a specific target audience. Here's a step-by-step guide to finding your blogging niche:

Start by listing your passions, hobbies, and areas of expertise. Consider what topics you enjoy discussing and researching. Think about what you could write about consistently without losing interest. Use tools like Google Trends, keyword research tools, and social media to gauge the popularity and search volume of potential niche topics. Look for a balance between your interests and topics that have a substantial audience.

Even in popular niches, finding a unique angle or perspective can help you stand out. Consider how you can add value or present information differently. Your personal experiences, expertise, and viewpoint can shape your niche's uniqueness. Research existing blogs in your potential niche. Are there established bloggers? What kind of content are they producing? Analyze their strengths and weaknesses to identify gaps you can fill or areas where you can provide a better experience.

Choose a niche with potential for long-term growth and relevance. Avoid niches that might become obsolete quickly. Evergreen topics (those that remain relevant over time) are often a safer bet. Define your target audience's demographics, interests, pain points, and needs. Tailor your niche to resonate with this audience, addressing their specific concerns and offering valuable solutions. Ensure your chosen niche aligns with your genuine passion and interest. Blogging requires dedication, so you'll be more likely to stay motivated if you love your niche.

Before committing fully, create a few test blog posts to gauge your interest and audience response. Pay attention to engagement, comments, and traffic to assess the potential of your chosen niche. Keep in mind that your niche can evolve over time as you gain more insights and feedback. Be open to adapting your focus based on what resonates most with your audience. If your initial niche seems broad, consider niching down further to target a more specific subtopic. A narrower niche can help you establish authority and attract a dedicated audience.

Finding your blogging niche involves a balance between your interests, market demand, and unique angle. Choose a niche that resonates with you, addresses a specific audience's needs, and has potential for growth. Your niche is a foundation upon which you'll build your blog, so take your time to research, and select the right direction. Remember that your chosen niche should be a source of inspiration and motivation as you embark on your blogging journey.

Identifying Your Passion And Expertise

Identifying your passion and expertise is a critical step in determining the right niche for your blog. Your passion fuels your motivation, while your expertise ensures the quality and value of your content. Here's how to identify your passion and expertise:

Take some time to reflect on your interests, hobbies, and the topics that genuinely excite you. Consider what you could talk about for hours without getting bored. Make a list of skills you've acquired over the years. These could be related to your profession, hobbies, education, or personal experiences. Think about the topics your friends, family, or colleagues often seek your advice on. This could indicate areas where you have expertise.

Consider your career and educational background. Are there specialized areas within your field that you're particularly knowledgeable about? Explore the subjects you enjoy learning about in your free time. If you're naturally curious about a topic, it might make a great niche. Consider activities that bring you joy and fulfillment. Your hobbies, whether it's cooking, traveling, photography, fitness, or DIY projects, can provide excellent niches.

Unique life experiences, challenges you've overcome, or journeys you've embarked on can set you apart and become a foundation for your blog. Examine the books, magazines, podcasts, and online content you consume regularly. Your preferences can reveal your passions. Look for an overlap between your passion and expertise. Finding a balance between what you love and what you're good at ensures both enthusiasm and quality in your content.

After identifying potential niches based on passion and expertise, research the market demand for those topics. Check online forums, social media, and keyword research tools to gauge interest. Keep in mind that expertise doesn't mean knowing everything from the start. You can develop your expertise over time through continuous learning and research. If you're torn between a few options, consider creating test content for each niche. Monitor your own excitement while creating the content and the engagement it receives from your audience. Passion drives your commitment and resilience in the face of challenges. It's what will keep you motivated to consistently produce high quality content.

Identifying your passion and expertise is the foundation of a successful blog. Choosing a niche that aligns with both will make your blogging journey enjoyable and fulfilling. Remember that your passion and expertise can evolve over time, so don't be afraid to refine your niche or adapt as you learn and grow as a blogger.

Researching And Evaluating Potential Niches

Researching and evaluating potential niches is a crucial step in finding the right focus for your blog. Thorough research ensures that your chosen niche has an audience, demand, and potential for growth. Here's how to effectively research and evaluate potential niches:

Start by brainstorming a list of topics that align with your interests, passions, and expertise. Don't worry about filtering at this stage; jot down as many ideas as you can. Use keyword research tools like Google Keyword Planner, Ubersuggest, or Ahrefs to analyze the search volume and competition for keywords related to your potential niches. High search volume indicates a strong demand for content in that niche.

Research existing blogs and websites in the niches you're considering. Analyze the quality of their content, engagement (comments, social shares), and their audience size. Define your target audience's demographics, interests, pain points, and preferences. Ensure your chosen niche resonates with this audience and addresses their needs. Explore forums, social media groups, and online communities related to your potential niches. Participate in discussions to understand the questions, concerns, and topics that are most relevant to the audience.

Evaluate the potential for creating diverse and engaging content within the niche. A niche with various angles, subtopics, and formats can keep your content fresh and interesting. Research how bloggers in similar niches monetize their blogs. Are there affiliate programs, sponsored content opportunities, or products you can create and sell? Consider whether the niche has the potential to remain relevant and sustainable over time. Avoid niches that might become obsolete quickly. Ensure your chosen niche aligns with your passion and expertise. Your genuine interest will translate into authentic and engaging content.

Check for any upward or downward trends in the niche using tools like Google Trends. A consistent or growing interest suggests a niche with long-term potential. Create a few sample blog posts or pieces of content within each potential niche. This can help you gauge your interest in creating content and assess audience engagement. Trust your intuition. If you feel genuinely excited and motivated about a particular niche, it's likely a good fit for you. Consider if the niche allows room for growth and expansion over time. As your blog evolves, you might want to cover related topics to keep your content fresh.

Thorough research and evaluation are key to selecting a niche that aligns with your passion, has a target audience, and offers potential for growth. Take the time to analyze market demand, competition, and audience preferences. By making informed decisions, you'll increase your chances of creating a successful and engaging blog that resonates with readers.

Choosing The Perfect Niche For Long-Term Success

Selecting a niche that ensures long-term success for your blog requires careful consideration and strategic planning. Here's a step-by-step approach to help you choose the perfect niche that aligns with your goals and sustains your blogging journey over time:

Choose a niche that genuinely excites you and aligns with your personal interests and passions. Your enthusiasm will shine through in your content and keep you motivated over the long term. Research niches that have a substantial and consistent demand. Look for topics that people actively search for. Identify audience pain points and needs that your content can address effectively.

Study the competition within potential niches. Consider niches where there's a balance between demand and competition. Assess whether you can offer a unique perspective or fill gaps that existing blogs might have. Opt for niches that offer evergreen content opportunities. These are topics that remain relevant and valuable over time. Niches with timely content might be popular temporarily but could lose relevance quickly.

Evaluate the monetization potential of your chosen niche. Look for niches where you can diversify income streams, including affiliate marketing, sponsored posts, digital products, and more. Select a niche that aligns with your expertise, skills, and experiences. Your credibility and ability to provide valuable insights will contribute to your long-term success. Aim for a niche with the potential for audience growth and engagement. Check if there are active online communities, social media groups, or forums related to the niche.

Choose a niche that allows you to create diverse content formats, such as articles, videos, podcasts, and visuals. Diversification keeps your content fresh and caters to different audience preferences. Opt for a niche that offers room for growth and evolution. As you learn more about your audience and industry, you might want to expand your niche's scope. Think about whether you can see yourself consistently producing content in the chosen niche for years to come. Long-term success requires dedication and commitment.

Consider the niche's trends and future outlook. Is the niche likely to remain relevant and in demand in the coming years? Create a few test pieces of content within the chosen niche and monitor audience engagement and your own enthusiasm. This helps you validate whether the niche is the right fit for you.

Choosing the perfect niche for long-term success involves a combination of your personal passion, market demand, audience engagement, and monetization potential. It's a decision that requires thorough research, self-awareness, and a clear understanding of your goals as a blogger. By carefully considering these factors and making an informed choice, you can set the foundation for a successful and sustainable blogging journey.

CHAPTER 3: SETTING UP YOUR BLOGGING PLATFORM

Selecting the Right Blogging Platform

Domain Name Selection and Registration

Customizing Your Blog's Design and Layout

Setting Up Your Blogging Platform

Setting up your blogging platform is a crucial step in launching your blog. The platform you choose will influence your blog's design, functionality, and ease of use. Here's a step-by-step guide to help you set up your blogging platform:

Select a platform that suits your needs and technical comfort level. Popular options include WordPress, Blogger, and Medium. WordPress.org offers more control and customization options, while WordPress.com is a hosted solution. Choose a domain name that reflects your blog's topic and is easy to remember. Register your domain through a domain registrar or your chosen blogging platform. If you're using WordPress.org, you'll need a hosting service to make your blog accessible on the internet. Research and choose a reputable hosting provider that offers good speed, uptime, and customer support.

If you're using WordPress.org, most hosting providers offer one click WordPress installation. Follow the provider's instructions to install WordPress on your domain. Choose a theme that matches your blog's style and niche. You can find both free and premium themes. Customize the theme's appearance, colors, typography, and layout to create a unique look. Install essential plugins to enhance your blog's functionality, security, and SEO. Some popular plugins include Yoast SEO, Akismet (for spam protection), and Jetpack.

Create essential pages such as "About," "Contact," and a "Privacy Policy" page. These pages provide important information and establish your blog's credibility. Set up SEO-friendly permalinks (URL structure) that include relevant keywords. This improves your blog's search engine visibility. Create relevant categories and tags for your blog posts to organize content and make navigation easier for readers. Start creating and publishing high quality, valuable content that aligns with your chosen niche. Format your content using headings, subheadings, images, and other multimedia elements.

Use an SEO plugin to optimize your content for search engines. Focus on optimizing titles, Meta descriptions, and using relevant keywords. Ensure your blog is responsive and displays properly on various devices, including desktops, tablets, and smartphones. Set up Google Analytics to track your blog's performance, including traffic, behavior, and engagement. Check your blog's load speed and make any necessary optimizations. A fast loading website improves experience and SEO rankings. Start promoting your blog on social media, forums, and other relevant platforms to attract initial readership.

Setting up your blogging platform is an exciting step that lays the foundation for your blog's success. By choosing the right platform, customizing it to your needs, and creating valuable content, you can create a professional and engaging blog that resonates with your target audience.

Selecting The Right Blogging Platform

Choosing the right blogging platform is crucial for the success and ease of managing your blog. Different platforms offer varying levels of customization, features, and control. Here's a breakdown of some popular blogging platforms to help you make an informed decision:

WordPress.org

Pros: Highly customizable, offers thousands of themes and plugins, provides full control over your blog, excellent for SEO optimization, can be used to create any type of website.

Cons: Requires separate hosting and domain registration, some technical knowledge might be necessary, managing updates and security is your responsibility.

Best For: Those seeking complete control, flexibility, and scalability for their blog or website.

WordPress.com

Pros: Hosted solution, friendly interface, no need for separate hosting or domain, handles updates and security, offers free and premium plans.

Cons: Limited customization compared to self-hosted WordPress, restrictions on certain plugins and themes, less control over your site.

Best For: Beginners or casual bloggers who want a simpler setup and don't need extensive customization.

Blogger

Pros: Owned by Google, easy to set up and use, no hosting or domain expenses, integration with Google services, suitable for simple blogs.

Cons: Limited customization and features, outdated interface, fewer design options, Google can suspend your blog without notice for policy violations.

Best For: Those looking for a straightforward, no-frills blogging platform.

Medium

Pros: friendly, clean and minimalist design, built-in audience and exposure, easy social sharing, no technical setup required.

Cons: Limited customization options, no control over the platform, monetization options is limited.

Best For: Writers who want a hassle-free platform with built-in readership and a focus on content.

Wix

Pros: Drag-and-drop website builder, suitable for beginners with no technical skills, offers various templates and design options.

Cons: Limited scalability for complex websites, might encounter limitations in customization, may not be as SEO-friendly.

Best For: Beginners who prioritize ease of use and visual design.

Squarespace

Pros: friendly, visually appealing templates, suitable for artists, photographers, and creative professionals, includes hosting and domain.

Cons: Limited flexibility compared to self-hosted platforms, fewer third-party integrations, might be more expensive.

Best For: Creative professionals who want an aesthetically pleasing platform without delving into technical complexities.

Ghost

Pros: Designed specifically for bloggers, clean and minimalist interface, focused on writing experience, offers built-in SEO tools.

Cons: Fewer customization options compared to WordPress, might require more technical knowledge for setup.

Best For: Writers and bloggers who prioritize a distraction free writing environment and strong SEO.

The choice of a blogging platform depends on your technical comfort level, customization needs, future plans for your blog, and the level of control you desire. WordPress.org is a versatile option for those seeking complete control and scalability, while WordPress.com and other platforms offer simplicity and ease of use. Evaluate the pros and cons of each platform to determine which aligns best with your goals and vision for your blog.

Domain Name Selection And Registration

Choosing the right domain name is a crucial step in establishing your online presence. It's the web address where visitors will find your blog. Here's a guide on how to select and register a domain name:

Your domain name should ideally reflect the main topic or focus of your blog. It should give visitors an idea of what to expect from your content. Choose a domain name that is concise, easy to remember, and not too complicated to spell. Avoid long, complex, or hyphenated domain names. Ensure your chosen domain name doesn't infringe on trademarks or copyrights of existing brands or businesses. Common extensions include .com, .net, and .org. Choose an extension that suits the nature of your blog and is easy to remember.

Incorporate relevant keywords if possible, but avoid keyword stuffing. A domain name with relevant keywords can contribute to your blog's search engine ranking. If you're building a personal brand or intend to expand beyond just blogging, consider using your own name as the domain. Use domain registration services or domain registrars to check if your desired domain name is available. Have a few backup options in case your preferred name is taken.

Numbers and special characters can be confusing when spoken aloud and are often mistyped. Ensure that the same or similar name is available on major social media platforms. Consistent branding across platforms helps with recognition. Once you've settled on a domain name, register it through a domain registrar. Popular registrars include GoDaddy, Namecheap, Google Domains, and more. Consider adding privacy protection to your domain registration. This shields your personal contact information from being publicly visible in the WHOIS database.

Be aware of the domain renewal fees and renewal periods associated with your chosen registrar. Set up reminders for domain renewal to avoid unintentional expiration and potential loss of your domain. Understand the domain transfer policies of your chosen registrar in case you decide to switch providers in the future. Choose a domain name that will remain relevant and suitable as your blog grows and evolves.

Your domain name is an essential part of your blog's identity. Take your time to choose a domain that aligns with your content, is memorable, and is easy to promote. Register your domain with a reputable registrar, and ensure you understand the terms and renewal process. A well-chosen domain name can contribute significantly to the success and recognition of your blog.

Customizing Your Blog's Design And Layout

Customizing the design and layout of your blog is essential to creating a visually appealing and friendly experience for your readers. Here's a step-by-step guide to help you customize your blog's design and layout:

Select a theme that matches your blog's niche and style. Many blogging platforms offer a range of free and premium themes. Look for a theme with the features and layout you desire. Most themes allow you to customize colors, fonts, and typography to match your brand or personal preferences. Choose colors that are visually pleasing and easy to read. Ensure font choices are legible. Upload a header image that represents your blog's theme or niche. Consider adding a logo if applicable. The header is often the first thing visitors see, so make it engaging and reflective of your content.

Create a friendly navigation menu that helps visitors find different sections of your blog. Include essential pages like "Home," "About," "Contact", and categories if applicable. Customize your sidebar with useful widgets like search, recent posts, categories, social media links, and an email subscription form. Widgets enhance navigation and encourage engagement. Customize your homepage layout to showcase your most important content. Choose whether you want a static homepage or a dynamic feed of your latest blog posts.

Some themes allow you to feature specific posts, products, or images in a slider or grid format on your homepage. Use this feature to highlight your best content. Customize your footer with relevant information, such as copyright notice, contact details, and links to important pages. Footer widgets can also provide additional navigation options. Optimize images for web to ensure fast loading times and a seamless experience. Compress images and use alt text for accessibility and SEO.

Ensure your blog's design is responsive, meaning it adapts to different screen sizes and devices. Test your blog on various devices to ensure it looks and functions well. Use the preview function to see how changes to your design will appear before making them live. Test different layouts and elements to find the best combination. Regularly review and update your blog's design to keep it fresh and aligned with current design trends. Ensure your design remains cohesive with your content and branding. Ask friends, family, or your blog's early readers for feedback on your design and layout. Constructive feedback can help you identify areas for improvement.

Customizing your blog's design and layout allows you to create a unique and engaging visual identity that resonates with your audience. Take your time to explore different options, experiment with layouts, and ensure your design is friendly and responsive. A well-designed blog enhances the overall reading experience and contributes to the success of your blogging journey.

CHAPTER 4: CRAFTING COMPELLING CONTENT

Mastering the Art of Storytelling

Planning Your Content Strategy

Writing Engaging and Valuable Blog Posts

Crafting Compelling Content

Creating compelling content is at the heart of successful blogging. It's what keeps your readers engaged, encourages them to return, and attracts new audiences. Here's a comprehensive guide to help you craft compelling content for your blog:

Understand your target audience's preferences, interests, and pain points. Tailor your content to resonate with their needs and provide solutions. Every piece of content should offer value to your readers. Whether its information, entertainment, inspiration, or solutions, ensure your content serves a purpose. Offer a unique perspective or angle on your chosen topics. Stand out by presenting information in a way that's different from what's already available.

Craft attention-grabbing headlines that promise value or address a problem. A compelling headline encourages readers to click and read more. Hook readers from the start with an engaging introduction. Pose a question, share a personal story, or present a surprising fact. Organize your content with clear headings, subheadings, and paragraphs. Use bullet points, numbered lists, and visual elements to break up text and enhance readability.

Write well structured, error free content that demonstrates your expertise and professionalism. Edit and proofread your content to ensure accuracy and clarity. Incorporate relevant images, infographics, and videos to enhance your content's visual appeal. Visual elements can help explain concepts and make content more engaging. Use storytelling techniques to make your content relatable and memorable. Personal anecdotes and narratives create a connection with your readers.

Back your claims with credible research, data, and statistics. Well researched content establishes your authority and builds trust. Evoke emotions in your readers through stories, metaphors, and relatable content. Emotional connections can make your content more memorable. Address common problems and challenges your audience faces. Offer practical solutions and actionable advice.

Write content that's the right length for your topic. Long form content can provide in-depth insights, while shorter posts are quick and easy to digest. End your content with a clear call to action. Encourage readers to leave comments, share the post, subscribe, or take any desired action. Publish content consistently. Set a realistic posting schedule and stick to it. Consistency keeps your audience engaged and builds anticipation.

Encourage reader engagement through questions, polls, and discussions in your content. Respond to comments and engage with your audience to foster a sense of community. Pay attention to your content's performance. Analyze which topics resonate the most and adapt your content strategy accordingly.

Crafting compelling content requires a combination of understanding your audience, offering value, and delivering information in an engaging and unique way. Focus on quality, clarity, and providing solutions to your readers' needs. Over time, your consistently compelling content will establish your blog as a valuable resource and contribute to its long-term success.

Mastering The Art Of Storytelling

Storytelling is a powerful tool that can captivate your audience, convey your message, and make your content more relatable and memorable. Here's a guide to help you master the art of storytelling in your blog:

Begin your story with a captivating hook that draws readers in and piques their curiosity. Craft an opening that sets the tone and context of your story. Introduce the main characters or elements. Whether your story involves real people, fictional characters, or even concepts, develop them with relatable traits, emotions, and motivations. Describe the setting in which your story takes place. Use sensory details to immerse readers in the environment.

Use descriptive language and vivid imagery to paint a picture for your readers. Show emotions, actions, and scenes rather than just telling about them. Introduce a conflict or challenge that your characters face. This creates tension and keeps readers engaged. Provide a resolution or conclusion to your story, offering a satisfying outcome or lesson. Evoke emotions in your readers by creating situations that they can relate to on a personal level. Incorporate dialogue to bring your characters to life and add authenticity to your story.

Metaphors and analogies can help explain complex concepts by comparing them to something familiar. Use pacing and anticipation to build suspense, keeping readers engaged and curious about what happens next. Choose a tone that matches the mood of your story. Whether it's lighthearted, serious, or emotional, consistency is key. Reach a peak moment of tension and excitement in your story, often referred to as the climax.

Make your story relatable by highlighting universal themes, struggles, or emotions that your audience can identify with. If your story has a moral or lesson, make sure it's clear to your readers by tying it into the resolution. Once you've written your story, edit it for clarity, flow, and coherence. Trim unnecessary details and ensure the story stays focused on its core elements. Practice storytelling regularly. The more you practice, the more you'll refine your skills and develop your unique storytelling style.

Experiment with different types of stories, such as personal anecdotes, case studies, or fictional narratives. Ensure your stories are relevant to your blog's niche and audience. The stories should support the main message you want to convey. Mastering the art of storytelling can elevate your blog by making your content more engaging, relatable, and memorable. By incorporating well-crafted stories into your posts, you can create a stronger connection with your readers and convey your messages in a more impactful way.

Planning Your Content Strategy

A well-structured content strategy is essential for consistently producing valuable and engaging content for your blog. Here's a comprehensive guide to help you plan an effective content strategy:

Clearly define your goals for your blog. Are you aiming to educate, inspire, entertain, or promote products/services? Research your target audience's demographics, interests, pain points, and preferences. Create audience personas to guide your content creation. Determine the types of content you'll create, such as articles, videos, podcasts, infographics, and more. Variety keeps your content fresh and caters to different learning styles.

Decide how often you'll publish content. Consistency is key to keeping your audience engaged. Choose a realistic publishing schedule that you can maintain. Conduct thorough research on topics related to your niche. Identify trending topics, frequently asked questions, and areas with less competition. Create a content calendar to plan and organize your content schedule. Map out topics, publication dates, and any promotional activities.

Identify pillar content (comprehensive guides, in-depth articles) that serves as the foundation for your niche. Plan subtopics that expand upon these pillars. Use keyword research tools to find relevant keywords with decent search volume and low competition. Incorporate these keywords naturally into your content for SEO. Mix educational, entertaining, and inspirational content. Share personal stories, case studies, how-to guides, listicles, and more.

Write high quality, well researched content that provides value to your audience. Create content that aligns with your goals and resonates with your audience's needs. Encourage reader engagement by including calls to action (CTAs), questions, and prompts for comments. Respond to comments and foster a sense of community. Plan how you'll promote your content. Utilize social media, email newsletters, forums, and collaborations. Share your content across relevant platforms to reach a wider audience.

Use analytics tools to track the performance of your content. Monitor metrics like page views, engagement, social shares, and conversion rates. Based on analytics, adapt your content strategy. Identify what's working and what needs improvement. Continuously refine your strategy to better align with audience preferences. Balance evergreen content (timeless, always relevant) with timely content (current trends, news). Evergreen content provides long-term value, while timely content capitalizes on trends.

Consider guest posting on other blogs or collaborating with fellow bloggers. It expands your reach and builds relationships in your niche. Keep your long-term goals in mind. Your content strategy should align with your overall blog objectives. A well-planned content strategy ensures that your blog consistently delivers valuable, relevant, and engaging content to your audience. By understanding your audience, diversifying content types, and adapting based on analytics, you can create a strong foundation for your blog's growth and success.

Writing Engaging And Valuable Blog Posts

Writing blog posts that are both engaging and valuable is key to attracting and retaining readers. Here's a guide to help you craft content that captures your audience's attention and provides meaningful insights:

Create a headline that immediately grabs attention and hints at the post's value. Use strong language, numbers, and intriguing questions to pique curiosity. Begin your post with a captivating hook to draw readers in from the very beginning. Share a surprising fact, a relatable story, or a thought provoking question. Plan your post's structure with a clear introduction, main body, and conclusion. Use headings and subheadings to break up content and improve readability.

Quickly establish the value readers will gain from your post within the first few paragraphs. Make it clear how your post will solve a problem or fulfill a need. Expand on your hook and introduce the topic in more detail. State the main purpose of the post and the benefits readers will receive. Write in a clear, concise, and conversational style. Avoid jargon or overly complex language. Break down complex concepts into easily digestible explanations.

Incorporate relevant images, infographics, and videos to enhance your content's visual appeal. Visuals can help illustrate points and make your post more engaging. Share personal stories or anecdotes that relate to your topic. This adds a human touch and makes your content relatable. Support your points with data, statistics, and real life examples. Concrete evidence adds credibility and strengthens your arguments. Break up your content with subheadings and bulleted or numbered lists. This makes your content easier to scan and enhances readability.

Anticipate and address common questions or concerns your readers might have about the topic. Providing answers demonstrates your expertise and builds trust. Encourage reader engagement by posing questions, seeking opinions, or asking for personal experiences. Respond to comments to foster a sense of community. Offer practical and actionable advice that readers can implement right away. Step-by-step instructions are valuable to readers seeking solutions.

Summarize the main points and takeaways of your post in the conclusion. Reinforce the value readers have gained from reading your content. End your post with a clear and relevant call to action. Encourage readers to share the post, leave comments, subscribe, or take any desired action. Edit your post for grammar, spelling, and clarity. A polished post reflects professionalism and enhances readability. Ensure your post is easy to read on mobile devices by using short paragraphs and concise sentences.

Crafting engaging and valuable blog posts requires a combination of captivating writing, valuable insights, and a reader focused approach. Keep your audience's needs and preferences in mind as you create content that informs, entertains, and resonates with your readers. With practice and attention to detail, you'll be able to consistently produce high quality posts that keep your readers coming back for more.

CHAPTER 5: THE POWER OF VISUALS

Utilizing Images, Infographics, and Videos

Enhancing Your Posts with Visual Elements

Tips for Creating High quality Visual Content

The Power Of Visuals: Incorporating Multimedia

Incorporating multimedia elements into your blog posts can greatly enhance the reader experience, making your content more engaging, informative, and memorable. Here's how to harness the power of visuals by integrating multimedia into your blog:

Use relevant images to break up text and illustrate key points. High quality images can make your content more visually appealing and grab readers' attention. Create or include infographics to present complex information in a visually appealing and easily understandable format. Infographics are excellent for conveying data, statistics, and step-by-step processes. Embed videos to demonstrate concepts, showcase tutorials, or share personal experiences. Videos provide a dynamic element that can engage readers on multiple levels.

Embed slideshows or presentations to provide in-depth explanations or share visual content in a structured manner. Use GIFs and animations to add humor, demonstrate processes, or emphasize key points. These elements can make your content more interactive and enjoyable. Incorporate charts, graphs, and diagrams to visualize data and trends. Visual representations of information can make your content more informative.

Include screenshots to illustrate software processes, website navigation, or other technical details. Visual examples can make instructions clearer and more actionable. Experiment with interactive elements like quizzes, polls, and interactive maps. Interactive content encourages reader participation and engagement. Create photo galleries to showcase visual content in a visually organized manner. This is particularly useful for topics related to travel, photography, or design.

Use a combination of images, text, and other multimedia to tell a compelling visual story. Visual storytelling can create a powerful emotional connection with readers. Offer audio versions of your content for readers who prefer listening. Podcasts and audio content provide a convenient alternative to reading. Embed relevant social media posts, especially if they include valuable insights, quotes, or discussions related to your topic.

Ensure that all multimedia elements are accessible to all s, including those with disabilities. Provide alt text for images, captions for videos, and transcriptions for audio content. Ensure that multimedia elements complement your written content and contribute to the overall narrative. Avoid overwhelming your readers with too many visuals that distract from the main message.

Ensure that multimedia elements are optimized for mobile devices and don't slow down your blog's loading speed. Test all multimedia elements to ensure they display correctly and enhance the experience. Check for broken links or outdated content regularly.

Incorporating multimedia elements into your blog posts can significantly enrich the reader experience, making your content more engaging, informative, and enjoyable. By carefully choosing and integrating visuals, you can effectively convey your message, simplify complex topics, and create a more memorable connection with your audience.

Utilizing Images, Infographics, And Videos

Images, infographics, and videos are powerful tools for enhancing your blog's visual appeal and conveying information effectively. Here's how to effectively use each of these multimedia elements:

Images

- Choose high quality, relevant images that support your content and add visual interest.
- Use images to break up long blocks of text, illustrate concepts, and evoke emotions.
- Optimize images for web to ensure fast loading times without sacrificing quality.
- Add captions to images to provide context and enhance the reader's understanding.

Infographics

- Create or use infographics to present complex data, statistics, or step-by-step processes.
- Design infographics with a clear structure, using colors, icons, and visuals to convey information.
- Make sure the information is easy to understand at a glance.

Videos

- Embed videos to provide in depth explanations, tutorials, interviews, or demonstrations.
- Use videos to engage readers who prefer visual and audi-

tory learning styles.

- Keep videos concise and focused, addressing a specific topic or question.
- Use captions or transcripts for videos to make your content accessible to a wider audience.

Visual Storytelling

- Combine images, infographics, and videos to create a visual narrative that tells a story.
- Use a combination of media to engage readers emotionally and intellectually.

How to Guides

- Create video tutorials or step-by-step image guides to help readers understand processes or tasks.
- Visual guides are particularly effective for DIY projects, recipes, and technical instructions.

Data Visualization

- Use charts, graphs, and diagrams to present data and trends visually.
- Visualizing data makes it easier for readers to grasp complex information.

Interviews and Testimonials

- Incorporate video interviews or image testimonials from experts, customers, or influencers.
- Video interviews add a personal touch and enhance

credibility.

Explainer Videos

- Use videos to explain concepts, theories, or products in a dynamic and engaging way.
- Visual explanations can make complex subjects more accessible.

Photo Galleries

- Create photo galleries to showcase visual content related to travel, events, or product reviews.
- Galleries allow readers to explore images in an organized manner.

Consistency in Style

Maintain a consistent style in your images, infographics, and videos to create a cohesive visual identity for your blog. Ensure that all multimedia elements are mobile friendly and responsive, providing a seamless experience on different devices. Always give proper credit for images, infographics, and videos that you didn't create yourself. Respect copyright and licensing regulations.

Optimize your multimedia elements for SEO by using descriptive filenames and alt text. This helps improve your blog's search engine visibility. Use analytics tools to track engagement with your multimedia content. Analyze which types of visuals resonate best with your audience.

Effectively utilizing images, infographics, and videos can elevate your blog's content, making it more engaging, informative, and visually appealing. Each type of multimedia element serves a unique purpose, so choose the ones that best enhance your content's message and connect with your audience's preferences. When used strategically, visuals can significantly enhance the overall impact of your blog posts.

Enhancing Your Posts With Visual Elements

Incorporating visual elements into your blog posts can significantly enhance the overall reader experience, making your content more engaging and memorable. Here's a guide on how to effectively enhance your posts with visual elements:

Select visuals that align with your content and reinforce your message. Whether its images, infographics, or videos, ensure they add value to your topic. Use visuals to break up long blocks of text, making your posts easier to read and more visually appealing. Readers are more likely to stay engaged when content is visually balanced. Begin your post with a high quality featured image that encapsulates the essence of your content. This image can set the tone and encourage readers to delve into the post.

Incorporate charts, graphs, and diagrams to make data and complex concepts more understandable. Visual representations simplify information and enhance clarity. Include captions for images and visuals to provide context and highlight their relevance to your content. Captions can encourage readers to pay attention to specific elements. Create or include infographics to condense complex information into a visually engaging format. Infographics are shareable and can increase the virality of your content.

Embed relevant videos to offer additional insights, demonstrations, or expert perspectives. Videos provide a dynamic element that captures attention and adds depth to your content. If your content involves software tutorials or step-by-step instructions, use screenshots to guide readers visually. Screenshots can help readers follow along and achieve the desired outcome. If you're promoting products, showcase them with high quality images or videos that showcase their features and benefits. Visuals help potential buyers get a better understanding of what they're considering.

Use a series of images or visuals to tell a story within your post. Visual storytelling captures attention and engages readers emotionally. Incorporate interactive elements like polls, quizzes, or clickable images. Interactivity encourages reader engagement and participation. Stick to a consistent visual style throughout your blog posts to create a cohesive brand identity. Consistency builds recognition and trust with your audience.

Ensure that your visual elements are optimized for web to avoid slowing down your page loading speed. Compress images and videos without sacrificing quality. Provide alternative text (alt text) for images to make your content accessible to visually impaired readers. Caption videos and provide transcripts for those who can't access audio. Use analytics to track engagement metrics related to your visual elements. Analyze which types of visuals generate the most interaction and adjust your strategy accordingly.

Enhancing your blog posts with visual elements not only adds aesthetic appeal but also improves reader comprehension and engagement. By strategically incorporating images, infographics, and videos, you can effectively convey information, tell stories, and create a more immersive experience for your audience. Remember to balance visuals with text and optimize for both accessibility and loading speed to ensure your content is well received by all readers.

Tips For Creating High Quality Visual Content

Creating high quality visual content requires attention to detail and a focus on delivering valuable and engaging visuals to your audience. Here are some tips to help you produce topnotch visual content for your blog:

Plan Your Visual Strategy

Determine the types of visuals that best suit your content and audience. Create a visual style guide to maintain consistency in colors, fonts, and overall aesthetic. Invest in a good camera, whether it's a DSLR, mirror less, or even a smartphone with a quality camera. High resolution visuals capture more detail and look more professional. Natural light is your best friend. Shoot in well-lit areas or use diffused lighting for soft shadows. Avoid harsh, direct sunlight that can create strong contrasts.

Follow the rule of thirds for balanced composition. Imagine a grid with two horizontal and two vertical lines, placing key elements along these lines or their intersections. Experiment with angles and perspectives to create visually interesting shots. Use photo editing software like Adobe Photoshop or Lightroom to enhance your visuals. Adjust brightness, contrast, colors, and sharpness to improve the overall look. Use tools like Canva or Adobe Illustrator to create informative and visually appealing infographics. Keep them simple, organized, and easy to understand.

Plan your video content carefully, outlining the main points and shots you'll need. Use a stable tripod or gimbal to avoid shaky footage. For videos, create a storyboard that outlines each scene, shot, and dialogue. Storyboarding helps ensure a clear and cohesive visual narrative. Write a script for videos that require narration or dialogue. If using voiceovers, ensure clear pronunciation and engaging tone. Use video editing software to trim, arrange, and add effects to your footage. Pay attention to pacing, transitions, and audio quality.

If you're creating animations or graphics, use software like Adobe After Effects or tools like Vyond. Keep animations smooth and avoid excessive effects that might distract from the message. Resize images to fit your blog's layout and optimize them for web viewing. Compress images and videos to maintain quality while minimizing loading times. Let your personality shine through your visuals. Authenticity resonates with audiences. Avoid over editing or using too many filters that may make your visuals look unnatural.

Experiment with different visual formats and styles to see what resonates most with your audience. Continuously analyze engagement metrics to refine your approach. Keep learning about photography, design, and video production techniques. Consistent improvement will reflect in the quality of your visual content. Don't hesitate to collaborate with photographers, designers, or videographers if needed. Seek feedback from peers, readers, or professionals to gain valuable perspectives.

Creating high quality visual content requires a combination of technical skills, creativity, and a deep understanding of your audience's preferences. Whether you're producing images, infographics, or videos, remember that delivering value and engaging your audience should be your primary focus. With dedication and practice, you can consistently produce visual content that enhances your blog and resonates with your readers.

CHAPTER 6: BUILDING A LOYAL AUDIENCE

Defining Your Target Audience

Implementing Audience Engagement Strategies

Creating Consistent and Valuable Content for Your Readers

Building A Loyal Audience

Building a loyal audience is crucial for the long-term success of your blog. A dedicated following not only boosts your blog's visibility but also creates a sense of community and trust. Here's how to cultivate a loyal audience:

Publish valuable, high quality content on a consistent basis. Reliable content keeps your audience engaged and eager for more. Continuously gather insights about your audience's preferences, interests, and feedback. Tailor your content to address their needs and aspirations. Interact with your readers through comments, emails, and social media. Respond to questions, comments, and feedback to foster a sense of connection.

Let your personality shine through your content. Authenticity builds trust and relatability. Share personal stories, experiences, and opinions that resonate with your audience. Maintain consistent branding across your blog, social media, and other platforms. A unified brand identity helps your audience recognize and remember your blog. Provide resources, guides, or tools that offer extra value to your readers. This positions you as an expert and resource in your niche.

Offer exclusive content to your loyal readers, such as behind the scenes insights, premium articles, or discounts. Exclusive content rewards loyalty and encourages readers to stick around. Start an email newsletter to regularly connect with your audience directly. Share updates, exclusive content, and insights that are not available on your blog. Engage with your audience on social media platforms by responding to comments, sharing relevant content, and fostering discussions. Social media helps extend your reach and build a broader community.

Schedule regular Q&A sessions, live chats, or webinars to interact with your audience in real time. These interactions strengthen the bond between you and your readers. Collaborate with other bloggers, influencers, or experts in your niche. Guest posting on each other's blogs exposes you to new audiences and builds credibility. Encourage readers to share their experiences, insights, or creations related to your niche. This creates a sense of involvement and shared ownership of your community.

Recognize and appreciate your loyal readers through shout outs, special features, or giveaways. Show that you value their support and engagement. Continuously strive to improve your content, engagement, and overall experience. Regularly adapting to your audience's changing needs maintains their interest. Building a loyal audience takes time. Be patient and consistent in your efforts. Over time, your dedicated efforts will yield meaningful results.

Building a loyal audience requires dedication, authenticity, and a genuine commitment to meeting your readers' needs. By consistently delivering high quality content, engaging with your audience, and offering value beyond your blog posts, you can foster a community of loyal followers who not only return for your content but also become advocates for your blog.

Defining Your Target Audience

Defining your target audience is a crucial step in creating content that resonates, engages, and adds value to your readers. Understanding who your audience is helps you tailor your content to their specific needs and interests. Here's how to define your target audience effectively:

Conduct Market Research

Research your niche to understand its demographics, trends, and challenges. Identify existing blogs, websites, and influencers that cater to your niche. If you already have some readers, analyze their demographics, interests, and behavior. Use analytics tools to gather insights about your current audience. Develop detailed audience personas that represent your ideal readers. Include demographic information, interests, goals, challenges, and behavior patterns.

Determine the pain points, challenges, and needs your target audience faces. Your content should address these issues and provide solutions. Understand your audience's goals, aspirations, and what they're trying to achieve. Craft content that helps them progress toward these goals. Divide your audience into segments based on factors like age, gender, interests, and preferences. Tailor content to specific segments when appropriate.

Look deeper into psychographic factors like values, beliefs, and lifestyle. This understanding allows you to create more resonant content. Social media platforms often provide insights into your audience's demographics and behavior. Use these insights to refine your understanding of your target audience. Join forums, groups, and discussions related to your niche. Engage in conversations to understand your audience's viewpoints and concerns.

Use surveys and polls to gather direct feedback from your audience. Ask questions that help you better understand their preferences. Regularly analyze your blog's analytics to track which content performs well and resonates with your audience. Adjust your content strategy based on these insights. Your target audience might evolve over time. Stay open to adjusting your approach as you gain new insights.

Experiment with different types of content and approaches to see what resonates best. Continuously refine your content strategy based on results. Ensure that your content aligns with your audience's values, interests, and preferences. Authenticity and relatability build strong connections. It's better to have a dedicated niche audience than to try appealing to a broad but disengaged group. Specificity helps you stand out and build a loyal following.

Defining your target audience is essential for creating content that speaks directly to the needs and interests of the people you want to reach. By conducting research, creating audience personas, and continuously refining your understanding, you can tailor your content strategy to attract and engage the right readers, ultimately growing a loyal and dedicated audience for your blog.

Implementing Audience Engagement Strategies

Engaging your audience is vital for building a strong community and fostering meaningful connections. Here are effective strategies to implement audience engagement on your blog:

Ask open ended questions at the end of your posts to encourage readers to share their thoughts. Respond to comments promptly to show that you value their input. Write thought provoking content that encourages readers to share their opinions and engage in discussions. Create a safe and respectful space for differing viewpoints. Incorporate interactive elements like polls, quizzes, and surveys in your posts. Interactive content encourages active participation from your audience.

Be active on social media platforms where your audience hangs out. Respond to comments, shares, and messages to maintain a consistent online presence. Encourage readers to contact you via email for questions, feedback, or collaboration inquiries. Respond to emails in a timely and personalized manner. Host live Q&A sessions on social media or through webinars. Engage with your audience in real time, answering their questions and sharing insights.

Share personal stories and experiences that resonate with your audience. Authentic stories make you relatable and encourage readers to connect with you emotionally. Organize contests, giveaways, or challenges related to your niche. Encourage participation by offering valuable prizes and recognition. Encourage readers to share their experiences, creations, or opinions related to your niche. Showcase generated content on your blog to highlight your community.

Address reader questions and concerns in your content. This shows that you're listening and responsive to their needs. Set up a forum or discussion board where readers can connect with each other. A community forum fosters deeper engagement and interaction. Offer glimpses into your daily life, work process, and creative journey. Behind the scenes content humanizes you and makes readers feel more connected.

Include social sharing buttons on your blog posts to make it easy for readers to share your content. Sharing increases your reach and exposes your blog to new audiences. Regularly conduct surveys to gather feedback about your content, design, and overall experience. Use the feedback to make improvements based on your audience's preferences. Celebrate your blog's milestones and achievements with your audience. Milestone celebrations make readers feel like they're part of your journey. Incorporate images, videos, and graphics to make your content more visually appealing and engaging. Visuals capture attention and communicate messages effectively.

Audience engagement is a dynamic and ongoing process that requires active effort and a genuine commitment to connecting with your readers. By implementing these strategies, you can foster a sense of community, build stronger relationships, and create an environment where readers feel valued and excited to interact with your blog.

Creating Consistent And Valuable Content For Your Readers

Consistency and value are the cornerstones of a successful blog. To keep your readers engaged and coming back for more, follow these tips for creating content that consistently delivers value:

Know your readers' interests, needs, and pain points. Tailor your content to address their specific challenges and aspirations. Plan your content ahead of time using an editorial calendar. This ensures a steady stream of posts and helps you maintain consistency. Consistency is key. Stick to a regular posting schedule that works for you and your audience. Whether it's weekly, biweekly, or monthly, reliability builds reader trust.

Prioritize quality content over churning out posts. High quality content resonates more with readers and has a lasting impact. Identify common problems your audience faces and provide practical solutions. Valuable solutions establish you as a credible resource in your niche. Go beyond surface level information. Dive deep into topics to provide comprehensive insights. In-depth content demonstrates your expertise and keeps readers engaged longer.

Use a variety of content formats such as articles, guides, videos, podcasts, and infographics. Different formats cater to diverse learning preferences. Stay updated on industry trends and news to provide timely and relevant content. Addressing current topics enhances your blog's credibility. Create evergreen content that remains relevant and valuable over time. This type of content continues to attract readers long after it's published.

Always keep your readers' interests and needs at the forefront of your content creation. Your blog should be reader centric, offering solutions and insights they seek. Use images, infographics, and videos to enhance your content's visual appeal. Visuals break up text and engage readers more effectively. Include calls to action (CTAs) that encourage readers to leave comments, share, or engage with your content. Interaction fosters a sense of community and connection.

Research your topics thoroughly to provide accurate and up-to-date information. Cite reputable sources to enhance your content's credibility. Develop a unique voice and perspective that sets your blog apart. Originality attracts readers looking for fresh insights and perspectives. Pay attention to feedback and analytics to continuously improve your content strategy. Adapt and evolve based on what resonates best with your audience. Encourage readers to provide feedback on your content. This helps you understand their preferences and make necessary adjustments.

Consistency and value are the pillars of a successful blog. By understanding your audience, delivering high quality content, and continuously refining your approach, you can create a blog that not only attracts readers but also keeps them engaged and loyal over the long term. Remember, the key is to provide content that addresses your readers' needs, educates them, and adds value to their lives.

CHAPTER 7: EFFECTIVE PROMOTION AND DISTRIBUTION

Leveraging Social Media Platforms for Blog Promotion

Collaborating with Other Bloggers and Influencers

Optimizing SEO to Drive Organic Traffic

Effective Promotion And Distribution

Creating great content is just the first step. To reach a wider audience and maximize the impact of your blog posts, you need to promote and distribute your content effectively. Here's how to do it:

Share your blog posts on social media platforms where your audience is active. Use engaging captions, relevant hashtags, and eye catching visuals to attract attention. Send out email newsletters to your subscribers whenever you publish new content. Personalize your emails and provide a brief teaser to entice readers to click through. Participate in online forums, discussion groups, and communities related to your niche. Share your expertise and link to your blog posts when relevant.

Write guest posts for other blogs in your niche, including a link back to your own blog. This exposes your content to a new audience and builds backlinks. Partner with influencers or experts in your niche to promote your content. Influencers' endorsements can significantly boost your content's reach. Repurpose your blog posts into different formats such as videos, podcasts, infographics, or slideshows. Distribute these across various platforms to reach different audiences.

Optimize your blog posts for search engines with relevant keywords, Meta descriptions, and proper formatting. SEO helps your content rank higher in search results and attracts organic traffic. Consider using paid advertising on platforms like Google Ads or social media. Target specific demographics to ensure your content reaches your ideal audience. Include social sharing buttons on your blog posts to make it easy for readers to share your content. Encourage them to share if they find the content valuable.

Collaborate with other bloggers or content creators on joint projects or content series. Cross promotion exposes your blog to their audience and vice versa. Share your content in relevant LinkedIn groups, Facebook groups, and other online communities. Make sure to follow each group's rules and guidelines. Respond to comments on your blog posts, fostering engagement and discussion. Engaged readers are more likely to share your content with others.

Participate in podcasts, interviews, or webinars to showcase your expertise. Mention your blog and share links during these appearances. Regularly monitor your website analytics to track which promotion methods yield the best results. Focus your efforts on strategies that generate the most traffic and engagement. Consistency in promotion is as important as consistency in content creation. Continuously promote your evergreen content to keep attracting new readers.

Effective promotion and distribution amplify the impact of your content by reaching a wider audience. By leveraging social media, email marketing, collaborations, SEO, and various other strategies, you can increase your blog's visibility, attract more readers, and build a loyal following. Remember, the key is to share your content where your target audience spends their time and to provide value that encourages them to engage, share, and return for more.

Leveraging Social Media Platforms For Blog Promotion

Social media is a powerful tool for promoting your blog and connecting with your audience. Here's how to effectively leverage various social media platforms for blog promotion:

Identify the social media platforms where your target audience is most active. Focus your efforts on the platforms that align with your niche and content. Complete your profiles with relevant information, a clear bio, and a link to your blog. Use a consistent profile picture and cover image to reinforce your brand. Visual content like images, infographics, and videos tend to perform well on social media. Create eye catching visuals that encourage s to engage and click through to your blog.

Write captions that are concise, intriguing, and relevant to the content you're promoting. Use emotive language and ask questions to encourage interaction. Use social media scheduling tools to post at optimal times when your audience is most active. Consistent posting keeps your content visible and maintains audience engagement. Research and use relevant hashtags to increase the discoverability of your posts. Don't overdo it; a few well-chosen hashtags are more effective than many irrelevant ones.

Respond to comments, messages, and mentions promptly. Engaging with your audience fosters a sense of community and encourages more interaction. Use platforms like Instagram Live, Facebook Live, or Twitter Spaces to host live sessions. Discuss your blog topics, answer questions, and share insights in real-time. Share snippets or teasers of your blog content with a link to read the full post. This piques curiosity and encourages readers to visit your blog.

Share engaging stories and short videos on platforms like Instagram and Facebook. Stories are temporary and can create a sense of urgency to view your content. Partner with influencers or bloggers in your niche for content promotion. Influencers' endorsements can expand your reach to their followers. Participate in Facebook groups, LinkedIn groups, and Reddit communities related to your niche. Share your content when appropriate and engage in discussions.

Organize social media contests or giveaways that encourage users to engage and share your content. Make sure the rules require participants to interact with your blog or social media. Use social media analytics to track which types of posts perform best and when engagement is highest. Adjust your strategy based on the insights you gather. Maintain an authentic voice and brand identity across all your social media posts. Consistency builds recognition and trust.

Leveraging social media platforms effectively can significantly amplify your blog's reach and engagement. By creating visually appealing content, engaging with your audience, utilizing features like live sessions and stories, and collaborating with influencers, you can create a strong online presence that drives traffic to your blog and builds a loyal readership. Remember, each platform has its unique characteristics, so tailor your approach to fit the preferences and behaviors of your target audience on each platform.

Collaborating With Other Bloggers And Influencers

Collaborating with other bloggers and influencers can greatly enhance your blog's visibility, credibility, and audience engagement. Here's how to effectively collaborate for mutual benefit:

Look for bloggers and influencers who share a similar niche or target audience. Ensure their content and values align with yours to create authentic collaborations. Start by engaging with their content, leaving thoughtful comments, and sharing their posts. Building a genuine relationship lays the foundation for successful collaborations. Before reaching out, consider how you can provide value to them. Whether its guest posting, cross promotion, or a joint project, offer something beneficial.

Craft a personalized outreach message that explains the collaboration idea and its benefits. Clearly communicate how the collaboration will be mutually rewarding. Collaborate on creating content together, such as co-written blog posts, videos, or podcasts. Sharing expertise from both sides offers a unique perspective to your audience. Write guest posts for each other's blogs, showcasing your expertise to a new audience. Guest posts also build valuable backlinks and improve SEO.

Allow influencers to "take over" your social media or blog for a day. Their content can introduce you to their followers and add variety to your platforms. Create challenges or giveaways that involve multiple bloggers or influencers. Participants promote the event to their audiences, resulting in broader reach. Host webinars, live chats, or panel discussions with collaborators. Such events provide valuable insights to your audience and increase engagement.

Partner with bloggers or influencers on affiliate marketing campaigns. Promote each other's products or services and earn commissions on sales. Regularly share each other's content on social media platforms. This exposes your content to a wider audience and builds a sense of reciprocity. Collaborate with influencers who have a larger following to introduce your blog to a new audience. Their endorsement carries weight and can significantly boost your credibility.

Mention and link to each other's content within your blog posts. This encourages your readers to explore related content on their blogs. Keep track of the results and impact of your collaborations. Reflect on what worked well and how you can improve future collaborations. Communicate clearly, meet deadlines, and fulfill your commitments. Building a professional reputation enhances your chances of future collaborations.

Collaborating with other bloggers and influencers allows you to tap into new audiences, share expertise, and create engaging content. By fostering authentic relationships, offering value, and maintaining professionalism, you can form mutually beneficial partnerships that expand your reach, strengthen your blog's credibility, and offer fresh perspectives to your audience. Remember, successful collaborations are built on trust, respect, and a shared commitment to delivering quality content.

Optimizing Seo To Drive Organic Traffic

Search engine optimization (SEO) is crucial for driving organic traffic to your blog. By optimizing your content for search engines, you increase the visibility of your blog in search results. Here's how to effectively optimize your blog for SEO:

Identify relevant keywords that your target audience is searching for. Use keyword research tools to find high ranking and relevant keywords. Optimize each blog post for a primary keyword. Place the primary keyword in the title, headings, meta description, and throughout the content naturally. Create valuable, informative, and well-structured content. Content quality is a significant factor in search engine ranking.

Write compelling Meta titles and descriptions that accurately represent your content. Meta data should entice readers to click through from search results. Include internal links within your blog posts to connect related content. Internal links help s navigate your site and distribute link equity. Include authoritative external links to reputable sources that support your content. Outbound links enhance the credibility of your content.

Ensure your blog is mobile responsive and provides a seamless experience across devices. Mobile friendliness is a ranking factor for search engines. Optimize images, use caching, and choose a reliable hosting provider to improve loading speed. Slow loading sites can negatively impact experience and SEO. Create friendly and descriptive URLs that include the target keyword. Clear URLs help both s and search engines understand the content.

Use header tags (H1, H2, H3, etc.) to structure your content logically. Headers provide a hierarchy that makes it easier for search engines to understand your content. Optimize images by using descriptive file names and adding alt text. Alt text helps search engines understand the content of your images. Generate and submit a sitemap to search engines to help them index your content. Sitemaps provide a clear map of your site's structure.

Use SEO tools like Google Search Console and Google Analytics to track your site's performance. Monitor your keyword rankings and traffic to identify areas for improvement. Prioritize a friendly design, easy navigation, and relevant content. Positive experience contributes to higher search engine rankings. Keep up with search engine algorithm updates and best practices. SEO strategies evolve, so continuous learning is essential. SEO results take time to show. Be patient and persistent in your efforts. Consistent optimization efforts will yield long-term benefits.

Optimizing your blog for SEO is an ongoing process that requires a combination of technical strategies and focused practices. By incorporating relevant keywords, creating high quality content, improving site speed, and following best SEO practices, you can improve your blog's visibility in search results, attract more organic traffic, and establish a strong online presence.

CHAPTER 8: MONETIZATION STRATEGIES

Exploring Various Monetization Models

Affiliate Marketing and Sponsored Content

Creating and Selling Your Own Products or Services

Monetization Strategies For Your Blog

Monetizing your blog involves turning your content and audience into revenue streams. There are several effective strategies to consider:

Sign up for ad networks like Google AdSense or Mediavine to display ads on your blog. You earn revenue when visitors click on or view the ads. Promote products or services relevant to your niche using affiliate links. You earn a commission for every sale or action generated through your referral. Partner with brands to create sponsored posts or reviews. Brands pay you to feature their products or services in your content.

Create and sell ebooks, online courses, templates, or printables. Digital products capitalize on your expertise and offer value to your audience. Offer premium content or a membership area with exclusive resources for subscribers. Charge a recurring fee for access to these valuable resources. Leverage your expertise to offer consulting, coaching, or mentoring services. Provide one-on-one guidance to clients seeking personalized assistance.

Host virtual workshops, webinars, or master classes related to your niche. Charge attendees for participation and access to valuable insights. Launch an online store selling physical products related to your niche. This can include merchandise, handmade items, or products you curate. Accept donations from your audience through platforms like Patreon or Kofi. Offer perks or exclusive content to donors as a token of appreciation.

Leverage your blog as a portfolio to attract freelance writing, design, or other related gigs. Use your skills to generate income outside of your blog. Approach brands or businesses in your niche and offer ad space on your blog. You can negotiate rates and terms directly. Charge brands or other bloggers to publish guest posts on your blog. Ensure that the content is relevant and valuable to your audience.

Offer a tiered subscription model where readers pay for access to premium content. Different tiers can offer varying levels of exclusive content. Capitalize on your blog's authority to secure speaking engagements or workshop opportunities. These events can provide both exposure and revenue. License your blog content to other websites, publications, or platforms. Ensure that you retain ownership and receive compensation for its use. Often, a combination of monetization strategies can provide a more stable income. Diversifying your revenue sources can mitigate risks.

Choose monetization strategies that align with your blog's niche, audience, and goals. Keep in mind that monetization should enhance, not detract from, the value you provide to your readers. Building a loyal audience and consistently delivering valuable content are foundational to successful monetization. Experiment with different approaches, adapt as needed, and focus on creating a sustainable and profitable blog business.

Exploring Various Monetization Models

Monetizing your blog can involve various models and strategies. Here's an overview of different monetization models you can explore:

Display Ads: Use ad networks like Google AdSense or Mediavine to display ads on your blog. You earn revenue based on clicks or impressions.

Direct Ad Sales: Sell ad space directly to businesses or brands in your niche. You negotiate terms and rates directly with advertisers.

Promote products or services using affiliate links. You earn a commission for each sale or action generated through your referral.

Amazon Associates: Join Amazon's affiliate program and earn commissions for sales made through your Amazon links.

Partner with brands to create sponsored posts, reviews, or other content.

Brands pay you to feature their products or services, and you disclose the sponsored nature of the content.

Membership Sites: Offer premium content or resources behind a pay wall.

Subscription Boxes: Curate and sell subscription boxes related to your niche, sending products to subscribers on a regular basis.

Sell Digital Products: Create and sell ebooks, online courses, templates, printables, and other digital products.

Physical Products: Launch an online store to sell physical products, merchandise, or items related to your niche.

Offer certain content only to paying subscribers.

Users pay a onetime fee or a recurring subscription to access valuable content.

Use platforms like Patreon or Kofi to receive donations from your audience.

Offer perks or exclusive content to donors as a thank you gesture.

Offer consulting, coaching, or advisory services related to your niche.

Use your expertise to provide personalized guidance to clients.

Host webinars, virtual events, workshops, or conferences related to your niche.

Charge participants for attendance and access to valuable insights.

License your blog content to other websites, publications, or platforms.

Content syndication involves allowing your content to be republished on other platforms for a fee.

Capitalize on your blog's authority to secure speaking engagements or workshop opportunities.

Speaking fees can be a source of income and exposure.

Charge brands or other bloggers to publish guest posts or collaborate on content.

Ensure the content aligns with your niche and audience.

Set up a "Buy Me a Coffee" or similar button for readers who want to support your work with small donations.

Combine multiple monetization strategies to diversify your revenue streams.

Find a mix that works best for your blog and audience.

Selecting the right monetization models depends on your niche, audience, and the value you provide. Some models may work better than others for your specific circumstances. Remember, building a successful monetization strategy takes time and experimentation. Focus on providing value to your audience while finding ways to generate revenue that align with your blog's mission and goals.

Affiliate Marketing And Sponsored Content

Affiliate marketing and sponsored content are two popular monetization strategies that can help you generate revenue from your blog. Here's how each strategy works and some tips for implementing them effectively:

Affiliate Marketing

Affiliate marketing involves promoting products or services through affiliate links. You earn a commission for every sale or action made through the links you share. Here's how to make the most of affiliate marketing:

- Select products or services that align with your blog's niche and are of interest to your audience.
- Promoting relevant products enhances your credibility and increases the likelihood of conversions.
- Join reputable affiliate programs in your niche. Many companies and platforms offer affiliate programs.
- Look for programs with competitive commissions and good conversion rates.
- Always disclose that you're using affiliate links in your content.
- Transparency builds trust with your audience.
- Promote products you genuinely believe in and have personally used or vetted.
- Authentic recommendations resonate more with your audience.
- Write informative, honest, and compelling content about the products you're promoting.
- Focus on how the product addresses your audience's

needs and solves their problems.

Sponsored Content

Sponsored content involves collaborating with brands or companies to create content that promotes their products or services. You receive compensation for featuring the sponsored content on your blog. Here's how to navigate sponsored content effectively:

- Partner with brands that align with your blog's niche and values.
- The products or services should resonate with your audience.
- Ensure the sponsored content aligns with your usual tone and style.
- Readers should feel that the content is consistent with your blog's identity.
- Clearly disclose that the content is sponsored in compliance with legal and ethical guidelines.
- Transparency is crucial for maintaining trust with your audience.
- Craft high quality content that offers value to your readers.
- The sponsored content should provide insights, solutions, or entertainment.
- Maintain a balance between sponsored and non-sponsored content.
- Overloading with sponsored content can alienate your audience.
- Negotiate terms with brands, including compensation, content requirements, and disclosure expectations.
- Ensure both parties are clear on expectations.
- Ensure the content aligns with the agreed upon terms and delivers the promised value.

- Meeting expectations maintains your credibility.

Both affiliate marketing and sponsored content can be lucrative ways to monetize your blog. However, remember that maintaining your audience's trust and providing value should always be your top priorities. Choose partnerships and products that genuinely resonate with your audience, and be transparent about your affiliations and sponsorships. A balanced and authentic approach will help you build a successful monetization strategy while maintaining the integrity of your blog.

Creating And Selling Your Own Products Or Services

Creating and selling your own products or services is a powerful way to monetize your blog while leveraging your expertise and catering directly to your audience's needs. Here's how to effectively develop and market your offerings:

- Choose a product or service that aligns with your blog's niche and addresses a specific problem or need your audience has.
- Conduct market research to understand your audience's preferences and pain points.
- Validate your product or service idea to ensure there's demand.
- Create a high quality product or service that provides genuine value to your audience.
- Solve a problem or fulfill a desire your readers have.
- Consider whether your offering will be a digital product (e.g., ebook, course, templates) or a physical product.
- Choose the format that best suits your audience and resources.
- Outline your product or service and create a detailed plan.
- Put in the effort to create content, materials, or physical items that meet your quality standards.
- Research the pricing of similar products or services in your niche.
- Price your offering competitively while ensuring you cover your costs and make a profit.
- Develop a sales funnel that guides potential customers from awareness to purchase.
- Offer valuable content, lead magnets, and incentives to

attract and nurture leads.

- Create persuasive sales pages that highlight the benefits of your product or service.
- Use persuasive copy, testimonials, and visuals to encourage conversions.
- Choose a secure payment gateway to process transactions.
- Ensure a smooth and secure checkout process for customers.
- Utilize your blog and social media to market your product or service.
- Use relevant keywords, email marketing, and social media promotions.
- Offer excellent customer support to address inquiries, concerns, and issues.
- Positive customer experiences lead to repeat business and referrals.
- After customers purchase, offer complementary products or additional services.
- Upsells and cross sells increase the average transaction value.
- Gather feedback from customers to improve your product or service.
- Continuously iterate and enhance your offerings based on insights.
- Use scarcity tactics like limited time offers or discounts to create a sense of urgency.
- Encourage quick decision making and conversions.
- Ensure a seamless experience from browsing to purchasing.
- User friendly navigation and clear instructions are essential.
- Your product or service should genuinely provide value and solve problems for your customers.
- Positive customer experiences lead to word-of-mouth referrals.

Creating and selling your own products or services allows you to monetize your expertise and build a direct relationship with your audience. By understanding your audience's needs, developing high quality offerings, and effectively marketing them, you can establish a reliable revenue stream while enhancing your blog's value and credibility. Remember, a customer centered approach and a commitment to delivering value are key to successful product or service monetization.

CHAPTER 9:
ESTABLISHING YOUR
ONLINE AUTHORITY

Becoming a Thought Leader in Your Niche

Engaging with Your Readers and Responding to Feedback

Building Trust and Credibility over Time

Establishing Your Online Authority

Establishing yourself as an authoritative figure in your niche is essential for the long-term success of your blog. Here's how to build and maintain your online authority:

- Develop a deep understanding of your niche.
- Research thoroughly, stay up-to-date with trends, and continuously learn.
- Create well researched, informative, and valuable content.
- Offer insights, solutions, and actionable advice that benefit your audience.
- Publish content regularly and consistently.
- Consistency reinforces your authority and keeps your audience engaged.
- Share unique perspectives, insights, and ideas.
- Differentiate yourself from others in your niche.
- Share your opinions on industry trends and challenges.
- Position yourself as a thought leader by offering fresh insights.
- Focus on addressing your audience's problems and needs.
- Your solutions should be actionable and effective.
- Support your arguments with data, statistics, and credible sources.
- Use references to enhance the credibility of your content.
- Collaborate with influencers and experts in your niche.
- Guest posts, interviews, and collaborations enhance your credibility.
- Attend industry events, conferences, and webinars.
- Network with peers, experts, and potential collabor-

ators.
- Engage with your audience through comments, social media, and email.
- Building a community enhances your authority.
- Provide valuable free resources like ebooks, guides, or templates.
- Free resources showcase your expertise and attract a larger audience.
- Present real world examples of how your advice has worked.
- Case studies demonstrate your practical expertise.
- Share your journey, experiences, and challenges.
- Transparency builds authenticity and relatability.
- Tackle complex or controversial subjects with well researched arguments.
- Handling difficult topics can demonstrate your depth of knowledge.
- Seek feedback from your audience and adapt based on their needs.
- Continuously improving enhances your authority over time.
- Showcase awards, certifications, or achievements related to your niche.
- Recognitions add to your credibility.
- Write guest posts for reputable blogs and publications in your niche.
- Guest posts extend your reach and introduce your expertise to new audiences.
- While establishing authority, remain open to learning and adapting.
- Humility and a willingness to learn maintain your credibility.

Building online authority is a gradual process that requires a combination of expertise, consistency, and engagement. By consistently creating high quality content, networking with industry experts, providing value, and engaging with your audience, you can establish yourself as a trusted and authoritative figure in your niche. Remember that credibility takes time to build, so focus on delivering value and cultivating genuine connections with your audience and peers.

Becoming A Thought Leader In Your Niche

Becoming a thought leader in your niche involves establishing yourself as an authoritative and influential figure whose insights are sought after by your audience and peers. Here's how to position yourself as a thought leader:

- Develop an in-depth understanding of your niche.
- Continuously educate yourself and stay up-to-date with the latest developments.
- Offer unique viewpoints and insights that stand out.
- Share unconventional ideas and challenge the status quo.
- Create high quality, well researched, and informative content.
- Your content should provide solutions, answer questions, and address challenges.
- Consistently publish content that showcases your expertise.
- Regular publishing builds your authority over time.
- Share content that sparks discussions, debates, and critical thinking.
- Thought provoking content positions you as a leader of meaningful conversations.
- Respond to comments, emails, and social media interactions.
- Engaging with your audience builds a loyal community.
- Connect with other influencers, experts, and peers in your niche.
- Networking exposes you to different perspectives and expands your reach.
- Write guest posts for reputable websites and publications in your niche.

- Guest contributions introduce your expertise to wider audiences.
- Participate in webinars, podcasts, conferences, and panels.
- Speaking engagements enhance your visibility and authority.
- Conduct original research or share in-depth studies related to your niche.
- Research backed content establishes you as a credible source of information.
- Share personal experiences, successes, failures, and lessons learned.
- Authentic storytelling humanizes your expertise.
- Anticipate industry trends and share your insights.
- Predicting trends positions you as a forward thinking leader.
- Address common challenges in your niche and provide practical solutions.
- Solutions based content adds value and builds trust.
- Offer mentorship, coaching, or consulting services.
- Sharing your knowledge directly with others solidifies your authority.
- Collaborate on projects, webinars, or content with other thought leaders.
- Collaboration expands your reach and credibility.
- Stay curious and continue learning about your niche.
- Adapting to new information demonstrates your commitment to growth.
- Becoming a thought leader takes time and consistency.
- Patience is essential as you build your reputation over time.

Becoming a thought leader requires dedication, expertise, and a commitment to providing value to your audience and industry. By consistently sharing valuable insights, engaging with your audience, collaborating with peers, and staying at the forefront of your niche, you can establish yourself as a respected and influential thought leader. Remember that thought leadership is a journey, and your focus should be on making meaningful contributions and fostering genuine connections within your niche.

Engaging With Your Readers And Responding To Feedback

Engaging with your readers and responding to their feedback is crucial for building a loyal and active community around your blog. Here's how to effectively interact with your readers and create a positive relationship:

- Respond to comments, emails, and messages in a timely manner.
- Prompt responses show that you value your readers' input.
- Express gratitude for comments, feedback, and interactions.
- Show appreciation for your readers' time and engagement.
- Pose questions, prompts, or calls to action in your content.
- Encourage readers to share their thoughts and experiences.
- Address readers by their names and reference their comments.
- Personalization makes interactions more meaningful.
- Maintain a friendly and respectful tone in your interactions.
- Positive interactions create a welcoming atmosphere.
- Pay attention to readers' concerns, suggestions, and opinions.
- Show that you are open to understanding their perspective.
- Respond constructively to criticism and negative feedback.
- Acknowledge concerns and offer solutions or explan-

ations.
- Admit when you don't have all the answers.
- Transparency builds trust and authenticity.
- Craft content that invites readers to participate, such as polls or surveys.
- Interactive content encourages engagement.
- Highlight generated content, such as testimonials or success stories.
- Recognizing readers' contributions enhances their sense of belonging.
- Seek feedback from your audience on your content and blog.
- Demonstrating that you value their input can lead to meaningful insights.
- Engage with readers on social media platforms where your blog is promoted.
- Social media interactions extend your reach and engagement.
- Infuse your responses with humor and emotion when appropriate.
- Humor and emotion make interactions memorable and relatable.
- Host live Q&A sessions or AMAs (Ask Me Anything) on social media.
- Live sessions allow direct interaction and immediate responses.
- Consistently engage with your readers over time.
- Building relationships requires ongoing effort.
- Implement suggestions from readers when possible.
- Showing that you listen reinforces their impact on your blog.
- Analyze feedback to identify areas for improvement.
- Constructive feedback can lead to better content and experience.

Engaging with your readers and responding to their feedback builds a strong and loyal community around your blog. By actively listening, valuing their input, and fostering positive interactions, you create a space where readers feel heard and appreciated. This interaction not only enhances reader satisfaction but also provides you with valuable insights for improving your content and blog. Remember, meaningful engagement is a two way street that requires genuine interest and effort on your part.

Building Trust And Credibility Over Time

Building trust and credibility is a gradual process that is essential for the success of your blog. Here's how to establish and nurture trust with your audience over time:

- Consistently deliver high quality, valuable content.
- Reliable content builds a reputation for credibility.
- Be transparent about your intentions, affiliations, and disclosures.
- Transparency fosters authenticity and trust.
- Communicate openly and honestly with your audience.
- Honesty builds a strong foundation for trust.
- Showcase your expertise through well researched and informative content.
- Demonstrating your knowledge establishes credibility.
- Support your arguments with references and citations from reputable sources.
- Citing sources enhances your content's credibility.
- Address reader concerns, questions, and criticisms openly.
- Responding positively to feedback shows your willingness to improve.
- Share testimonials from satisfied readers or clients.
- Social proof reinforces your credibility.
- Develop a consistent personal brand that reflects your values and expertise.
- A clear personal brand builds trust over time.
- Demonstrate your commitment to your blog's niche over the long term.
- Consistency over time enhances credibility.
- Offer unique insights, thought provoking content, and industry analysis.

- Thought leadership positions you as an authoritative source.
- Collaborate with other experts in your niche.
- Association with experts boosts your credibility.
- Share real world case studies and examples of successful strategies.
- Practical examples demonstrate the effectiveness of your advice.
- If you make a mistake, admit it and take responsibility.
- Honesty in the face of errors strengthens trust.
- Ensure your website is secure with HTTPS and proper security measures.
- A secure website enhances trust.
- Encourage readers to share their success stories and experiences.
- Testimonials validate the impact of your content.
- Avoid click bait and sensationalist headlines.
- Reliable, factual content builds credibility.
- Adhere to ethical blogging practices, such as proper citations and avoiding plagiarism.
- Ethical behavior builds trust with your audience.
- Building trust takes time and consistent effort.
- Patiently nurturing your audience leads to long term credibility.

Building trust and credibility requires a combination of quality content, transparent communication, expertise, and consistent engagement. Over time, your commitment to providing value, authenticity, and reliability will create a loyal and trusting audience that sees you as a credible source of information. Remember that trust is earned through actions, not just words, so prioritize integrity in everything you do on your blog.

CHAPTER 10: OVERCOMING CHALLENGES AND SUSTAINING SUCCESS

Dealing with Writer's Block and Burnout

Adapting to Changes in the Blogging World

Long-term Strategies for Consistent Growth and Sustainability

Overcoming Challenges And Sustaining Success

While building and maintaining a successful blog is rewarding, it also comes with its share of challenges. Here's how to overcome common challenges and ensure the sustained success of your blog:

- Pace yourself and avoid overextending.
- Plan content in advance and consider outsourcing or guest posts.
- Consistently engage with your audience through comments and social media.
- Encourage discussions and respond promptly to feedback.
- Continuously create fresh, relevant, and valuable content.
- Explore new distribution channels and revisit your SEO strategy.
- Diversify your monetization strategies to reduce dependency on a single source.
- Monitor and analyze which strategies are most effective for your niche.
- Regularly update plugins, themes, and security measures.
- Backup your content and maintain a reliable hosting provider.
- Focus on your unique voice and value proposition.
- Continuously innovate and explore emerging trends in your niche.
- Prioritize self-care and set boundaries.
- Take breaks, delegate tasks, and avoid overworking.
- Stay informed about changes in search engine algorithms and social media platforms.

- Focus on high quality content and engagement to adapt to algorithm changes.
- Regularly evaluate your content's performance and engagement metrics.
- Adjust your content strategy based on what resonates with your audience.
- Keep learning and stay updated about developments in your niche.
- Adapt your content to address new trends and challenges.
- Plan a content calendar and stick to a consistent posting schedule.
- Batchcreate content in advance to maintain consistency.
- Address negative feedback professionally and constructively.
- Use criticism as an opportunity for improvement.
- Understand privacy laws and regulations relevant to your blog.
- Implement necessary measures to protect data.
- Explore new platforms and content formats to reach a wider audience.
- Repurpose content for different platforms to maximize visibility.
- Stay adaptable to changes in content consumption habits and online trends.
- Experiment with new formats, such as video or podcasts.
- Regularly revisit your blog's purpose and mission.
- Focus on topics that genuinely excite you to maintain your passion.

Overcoming challenges and sustaining success in the blogging world requires resilience, adaptability, and a genuine commitment to your audience. By addressing challenges proactively, staying connected with your readers, and continuously improving your strategies, you can navigate hurdles and ensure that your blog remains a valuable resource in your niche. Remember that persistence, creativity, and a willingness to learn are key factors in building a thriving and enduring blog.

Dealing With Writer's Block And Burnout

Writer's block and burnout are common challenges for bloggers. Here's how to overcome them and maintain your creativity and passion:

Dealing with Writer's Block

- Step away from writing and engage in activities that relax and recharge you.
- Write in a different setting, like a park or coffee shop, to stimulate new ideas.
- Write without a specific goal or structure to unlock creativity.
- Use mind maps to visualize ideas and connections.
- Read books, articles, and blogs related to your niche to spark inspiration.
- Write for a set period, like 25 minutes, and then take a short break.
- Write about anything that comes to mind, even if it's unrelated to your main topic.
- Plan the structure and main points of your upcoming posts.
- Write about a different aspect of your niche or a related topic.
- Start writing even if it's not perfect; you can edit later.

Dealing with Burnout

- Prioritize sleep, exercise, healthy eating, and relaxation.
- Establish clear work hours and stick to them.
- Step away from screens and engage in activities you

enjoy.

- Delegate tasks or outsource aspects of your blog to ease the workload.
- Plan regular breaks and vacations to disconnect from work.
- Remind yourself of your blog's purpose and the impact you're making.
- Explore new hobbies, interests, and experiences to rejuvenate your creativity.
- Reflect on what's causing burnout and adjust your approach.
- Talk to friends, family, or fellow bloggers about your feelings.
- Engage in mindfulness exercises, meditation, or yoga to reduce stress.

Writer's block and burnout are normal challenges that bloggers face. By implementing strategies to overcome them, you can maintain your creativity, passion, and mental wellbeing. Remember that taking care of yourself, setting realistic expectations, and seeking support are essential for long-term success and enjoyment in the world of blogging.

Adapting To Changes In The Blogging World

The blogging world is constantly evolving, and staying adaptable is key to your blog's continued success. Here's how to navigate changes effectively:

- Keep up-to-date with industry trends, technological advancements, and algorithm changes.
- Follow authoritative sources, attend webinars, and read industry news.
- Explore emerging platforms and adapt your content to new formats (e.g., videos, podcasts).
- Diversifying your content distribution expands your reach.
- Ensure your blog is mobile friendly, as many users access content from mobile devices.
- Adapt your SEO strategy to changes in search engine algorithms.
- Focus on intent, experience, and featured snippets.
- Create content that addresses your audience's evolving needs and challenges.
- Regularly assess your audience's preferences through surveys or analytics.
- Stay active on relevant social media platforms and adapt to changes in algorithms.
- Engage with your audience through posts, stories, and live sessions.
- Repurpose existing content into different formats or for different platforms.
- Reach new audiences while maximizing your existing content's value.
- Email marketing remains a reliable way to connect with your audience amidst changing algorithms.

- Invest in your personal growth by attending courses, workshops, and conferences.
- Adapt your skills and knowledge to stay relevant.
- Adjust your monetization strategies based on shifts in your niche and audience preferences.
- Be open to trying new revenue streams.
- Regularly review your blog's analytics to identify trends and areas for improvement.
- Data driven decisions help you adapt more effectively.
- Enhance your blog's experience by optimizing loading times, navigation, and readability.
- Connect with fellow bloggers, influencers, and experts in your niche.
- Collaboration helps you stay connected and learn from others.
- Be willing to adjust your content strategy, posting frequency, and topics based on audience response.
- Listen to your readers and consider their suggestions for improvement.
- Feedback guides your adaptations.
- As the blogging world changes, authenticity remains vital for connecting with your audience.

Adapting to changes in the blogging world requires a combination of staying informed, embracing new opportunities, and maintaining a flexible mindset. By continuously learning, experimenting with new approaches, and prioritizing your audience's needs, you can ensure that your blog remains relevant and successful even in the face of evolving trends. Remember that adaptability is a valuable skill that can help you navigate the ever changing digital world.

Long-Term Strategies For Consistent Growth And Sustainability

Sustaining consistent growth and long term sustainability for your blog requires a combination of strategic planning, quality content, and continuous engagement. Here are strategies to ensure your blog's success over the long run:

- Set specific, measurable, achievable, relevant, and time bound (SMART) goals for your blog's growth.
- Create a comprehensive content plan that includes topics, formats, and a posting schedule.
- Address your audience's needs, preferences, and challenges.
- Focus on creating high quality content that provides value to your readers.
- Well researched and well written articles build credibility and retain readers.
- Collect email addresses and use email marketing to engage and retain your audience.
- Regular newsletters keep readers informed and connected.
- Respond to comments, encourage discussions, and build a sense of community.
- Engaged readers are more likely to become loyal followers.
- Continuously optimize your content for search engines to increase organic traffic.
- SEO ensures your blog remains discoverable over time.
- Incorporate a mix of text, images, videos, infographics, and interactive content.
- Diversification keeps your content fresh and appeals to different learning styles.

- Monitor industry trends and adjust your content to address current interests.
- Trend relevant content enhances your blog's relevancy.
- Collaborate with influencers, other bloggers, and experts in your niche.
- Networking expands your reach and brings new perspectives.
- Stay updated with the latest techniques, tools, and best practices in blogging.
- Ongoing learning keeps your strategies effective.
- Optimize your blog's design, navigation, and mobile responsiveness.
- A positive experience encourages repeat visits.
- Regularly analyze your blog's performance using metrics like traffic, engagement, and conversion rates.
- Data driven insights guide your growth strategies.
- Explore multiple monetization strategies to reduce dependency on a single source of revenue.
- Multiple streams increase your income stability.
- Regularly update and improve your older articles to keep them relevant and valuable.
- Refreshing content can boost its search engine rankings.
- Maintain your unique voice and authenticity in your content and interactions.
- Authenticity builds a loyal readership.
- Regularly assess your strategies and adapt based on what's working best.
- Flexibility allows you to pivot when necessary.
- Sustainable growth takes time. Stay committed even during slower periods.
- Acknowledge and celebrate your blog's achievements and milestones with your audience.

Consistent growth and sustainability require a holistic approach that combines strategic planning, quality content, audience engagement, and adaptation. By focusing on providing value, staying informed, and fostering a strong connection with your readers, you can build a blog that not only grows over time but also maintains its impact and relevance in your niche. Remember that the journey to long term success is a marathon, not a sprint, so patience, dedication, and continuous improvement are key.

AFTERWORD

Congratulations, dear reader, on completing "Blogging: Your Path to Success." As you turn the final pages of this book, I want to extend my heartfelt gratitude for joining me on this journey through the world of blogging and digital success.

The act of blogging goes beyond mere keystrokes; it's about leaving a mark on the digital canvas, sharing your thoughts with the world, and making a genuine impact. I hope this book has not only equipped you with the tools and strategies to thrive but also ignited a spark of inspiration within you.

Remember, success in blogging is not defined solely by metrics or numbers. It's about the connections you forge, the stories you share, and the lives you touch. Every word you write has the potential to shape perspectives, spark conversations, and create change.

As you continue your blogging journey, embrace your authenticity and let your passion guide you. The online world is vast, and the possibilities are endless. Stay curious, stay dedicated, and most importantly, stay true to your voice.

Whether you're a seasoned blogger reaching new heights or a

newcomer taking your first steps, know that your journey is unique, and your impact is significant. Keep evolving, keep learning, and keep contributing to the digital world.

Thank you for choosing "Blogging: Your Path to Success" as a companion on your blogging adventure. I'm excited to see how your journey unfolds and the stories you'll share with the world.

Wishing you a path of growth, fulfillment, and boundless success.

Warm regards,

Ali Muattar

Author, "Blogging: Your Path to Success"

ACKNOWLEDGEMENT

Completing "Blogging: Your Path to Success" has been a journey filled with growth, learning, and inspiration. I am deeply grateful to the individuals and organizations that have supported and guided me along this path.

First and foremost, I extend my heartfelt gratitude to my family and friends for their unwavering support, encouragement, and belief in my vision. Your presence in my life has been my anchor, and I am blessed to have you by my side.

I am indebted to my mentors and colleagues who have shared their wisdom and expertise, helping me refine my understanding of the digital world. Your insights have been invaluable in shaping the content of this book.

To my readers and followers, thank you for being the reason I write. Your engagement, feedback, and enthusiasm drive me to continually strive for excellence. It's your hunger for knowledge and growth that fuels my dedication to empowering individuals in the digital world.

I extend my appreciation to the team at ANish Publications for their support in bringing this book to fruition. Your dedication to quality and excellence has made this endeavor a true pleasure.

Finally, to every blogger and digital enthusiast who seeks to make their mark in the online world – this book is dedicated to you. Your passion, creativity, and commitment to authenticity inspire me every day.

As you travel on your journey toward blogging success, remember that the paths we tread are illuminated by the light of those who stand beside us. Each connection we make, each lesson we learn, and each story we share enriches our lives in ways beyond measure.

Thank you for being a part of my journey, and I hope "Blogging: Your Path to Success" guides you toward a future filled with achievement, fulfillment, and joy.

Warm regards,

Ali Muattar

Author, "Blogging: Your Path to Success"

ABOUT THE AUTHOR

Ali Muattar

Ali Muattar is a seasoned blogger, entrepreneur, and digital strategist with a passion for empowering individuals, and businesses to harness the full potential of the online world. His journey began with a single blog post that ignited a flame of curiosity and creativity, propelling him into the dynamic world of digital communication.

With over one and a half decade of experience, Ali has built a reputation as a thought leader in the worlds of blogging, content creation, and digital marketing. His blogs have reached millions, inspiring readers around the globe to discover their unique voices and share their stories.

Ali's entrepreneurial spirit led him to launch successful online ventures, each built on the foundation of authentic engagement and meaningful connections. He understands the pulse of the digital audience, recognizing the power of storytelling to captivate hearts and minds.

Beyond his role as a blogger and entrepreneur, Ali is a dedicated mentor, speaker, and educator. He has empowered countless individuals to break through digital barriers, guiding them toward success with actionable insights and motivational guidance.

When he's not crafting content or strategizing for his ventures, Ali enjoys immersing himself in books, exploring new cuisines, and indulging in outdoor adventures. He believes in the power of continuous learning and cherishes the connections he forges with fellow creators and dreamers.

"Blogging: Your Path to Success" is Ali's latest contribution to the world of digital enlightenment. He invites readers to join him on a transformative journey, where the art of blogging becomes a catalyst for personal growth, community building, and impactful change.

Connect with Ali Muattar online and stay tuned for his ongoing efforts to equip individuals with the tools and mindset needed to thrive in the ever evolving digital world.

Website: www.alimuattar.com
Twitter: @AliMuattar1
Instagram: @AliMuattar
LinkedIn: Ali Muattar

www.ingramcontent.com/pod-product-compliance
Lightning Source LLC
LaVergne TN
LVHW051741050326
832903LV00029B/2654